Na Walk

by April Reign
illustrated by Stephen Lewis

HOUGHTON MIFFLIN   BOSTON

Copyright © by Houghton Mifflin Company. All rights reserved.

No part of this work may be reproduced or transmitted in any form or by any means, electronic or mechanical, including photocopying or recording, or by any information storage or retrieval system without the prior written permission of Houghton Mifflin Company unless such copying is expressly permitted by federal copyright law. Address inquiries to School Permissions, Houghton Mifflin Company, 222 Berkeley Street, Boston, MA 02116.

Printed in China

ISBN 10: 0-618-88695-8
ISBN 13: 978-0-618-88695-1

14 15 16 17 18 0940 20 19 18 17 16 15
4500534889

On Monday, Mr. Hing took his class on a nature walk. He asked the children to look for things to measure. Mr. Hing gave each of them big paper clips or crayons.

Anita found a mushroom. She stood a paper clip next to it. The mushroom was just about as tall as the clip. She drew the mushroom in her notebook and wrote its measurement.

Read • Think • Write How tall was the mushroom?

Marco found a worm. Before it could wiggle away, he measured it. The worm was about 2 clips long. Marco also measured it with a crayon.

Read • Think • Write What were Marco's measurements?

Peter used crayons to measure the length of a feather. It was just a little bit longer than 3 crayons.

Read • Think • Write About how many crayons long was the feather?

Near the end of the walk, Meesha found a flower. Halfway up the stem measured 2 crayons.

Read • Think • Write About how tall was the daffodil?

Back in the classroom, the class shared what they had measured.

Responding

Vocabulary

Ugh! Worms!

Show

Look at page 4. Draw a picture to show how long the worm is.

Share

Predict/Infer Talk about what the boy used to find the length of the worm on page 4.

Write

Look at page 6. Write about how the girl measured the flower.